JO MAY

The Boro

Now and Then

Copyright © 2022 by Jo May

All rights reserved. No part of this publication may be reproduced, stored or transmitted in any form or by any means, electronic, mechanical, photocopying, recording, scanning, or otherwise without written permission from the publisher. It is illegal to copy this book, post it to a website, or distribute it by any other means without permission.

First edition

This book was professionally typeset on Reedsy.
Find out more at reedsy.com

*To the memory of times gone by
and for tomorrow.*

Also for my wife Jan who's artwork is on the cover.

Contents

Acknowledgement	ii
Get Lost!	1
You've Never Had It So Good	3
Chat in a Northern Park	12
Water and Chips	20
All-Purpose SUV	30
Back to Our Roots	39
Post Apocalypse	46
Go On Then, One More	53
STOP PRESS	60
About the Author	64
Also by Jo May	66

Acknowledgement

Thanks to all the folk who have passed this way and made Littleborough special.

Get Lost!

... in the maze of an old duffer's mind ...

We returned to Littleborough after a break of about twenty-five years. First morning back I walked the dog at 6.00 AM and encountered a woman wearing a dressing gown and slippers. By chance, I was wearing my Rupert Bear pyjamas under a fleecy jacket. We bid each other a polite good morning and moved on, both smiling. There wasn't much else to do, really.

So, one thing hasn't changed - quirky encounters. But other things have ... technology, for example. My friend sent me a text message recently. In an effort to seize the technological high ground, he finished, 'I've sent this message from my new smartwatch.' My response: 'Wonderful. I'm replying using my rechargeable underpants.' At which point the conversation ended. He probably wondered if I was taking it seriously.

When we left Lancashire it was midget gems and skipping ropes; now it's nitrous oxide and vapes. From the latter, fruity nebulae float around like fluffy clouds. I recently passed a glass bus shelter engulfed in a sweet-smelling fog. From within I heard a hacking cough. Peering out of the gloom, a ghostly man who'd taken to the vape as part of his health drive.

Gone are hopscotch grids, telephone boxes and banks, all made virtually redundant by mobile phones. Gone also is somewhere to park, the gentleman's outfitters and the fishmonger. Instead, we have cafés, nail bars and beauty parlours - both human and dog. Did our old dog really need a shampoo and set? Or did we just chuck him in a lodge.

Littleborough gems include Hare Hill Park, the canal and the stunning countryside. Wonderful Hollingworth Lake takes vastly increased footfall in its stride. A constant stream of humanity marches forth. Further afield, Rochdale library abandoned its historic Grade II listed home in favour of a glass cube. The old swimming baths is now a German supermarket. Yorkshire Street and Drake Street look to have been ransacked by invading Vikings. The Town Hall car park is partially pedestrianized so there's now limited parking. Gracie Fields statue stands proud and defiant, right where I used to park my car.

My wife is happy to be reacquainted with old school friends (shh, one wears a dressing gown!). She is now of an age to join the Townswomen's Guild. In days gone by they would dispense tea and no-nonsense wisdom with a blue-rinse and twin set and pearls. Different today. The wisdom remains but the modern Guilder is a young-at-heart community stalwart more likely to be sporting pink streaks in her hair.

Sure, Littleborough has changed. It's busier, faster and more fraught but there are still gems and plenty to enjoy. We are adapting and realize the town is still a rather nice place. Here follows one chap's efforts to get up to speed with today's world.

You've Never Had It So Good

2015

A Brief History

Jan and I have both lived in Littleborough, on and off, for 60+ years. We left Littleborough around 1990 and migrated to rural Shropshire, where we bought a wreck of a house. Ten years later it was just about fit to live in. Largely because we had low expectations. Then we built a boat, sold the house and lived in a marina on our boat. In effect we lived on a pond in the middle of a field (North Shropshire is basically one big, flat field). 'Pond life' my brother called us.

Why a boat all of a sudden? Basically, because Jan was given a very poor prognosis after two bouts of cancer. We needed to 'get on with life' so we took to the water. You can make just about anything - a house, money, etc. etc. but you can't make time. We believed ours was running out. I can tell you categorically that news like that changes your perspective. Ironically, and mercifully, our life-style choice probably saved Jan's life. We trundled around the canals of the UK for a couple of years then bought a knackered old barge and lived on the continent in a succession of places we'd never previously heard of.

So, for those not familiar, where is Littleborough? Well, Jan reckons it's under the staple. Every road atlas she's ever bought, Littleborough was always right in the centre of a double page under a rusty staple. (Road atlases - remember them?). Actually, it's in Lancashire in the foothills of the Pennines. Quite close to Yorkshire, but just far enough away not to be bothered by our age-old Wars of the Roses rival!

Back home

Trundling around in a boat we got there eventually. Travelling on the roads back home (2015), we seem to get nowhere fast. It's much busier, that's for sure. What follows is an impression of how things appear to a bloke who left in his prime and returned with less hair, dicky hips and diabetes. It's great to be back, but I do have the odd grumbly observation. Grumbling is a prerogative of (late) middle-aged people. Yes, I've joined the army of dithering buggers who can't keep up with the horrors of modern life.

We've come back to Littleborough where many golden nuggets wait to be discovered. The nuggets are often a bit damp, mind you, because in the foothills of the Pennines it rains a bit. To paraphrase Dudley Doolittle, local comedian, 'Littleborough is a great place to live; it would be wonderful if it had a roof.'

Increasingly aggressive motorists drive a tsunami of cars on clogged, crumbling highways. In places cobbles poke through decomposing tarmac. Ironically, the cobbles (or setts) are solid as a rock. In a perverse situation, motorways have become far more dangerous now they've added the prefix 'smart.' It's not easy to breach the speed limit because of the weight of traffic but the authorities have done their best to maximize revenue –

there are nearly as many speed cameras as cats eyes.

We also have to cope with those chevron things they've painted on the road, inverted sergeant's stripes that people invariably ignore. If we kept two between ourselves and the car in front we'd actually end up going backwards. The point is that if you leave the requisite gap, a 40-tonner from Eastern Europe squeezes in. Then you have to slow down to leave the requisite gap and another lorry sneaks in. Before you know it, you've reversed back to where you started!

Of course, there are alternative modes of transport. Trains, for instance. 'Sprinters' they imaginatively called them – but don't expect too much when the leaves are falling. Trains follow an imaginative timetable and seem to turn up when they feel like it. When they do, they are either empty or so packed that you can only sit down if you're pregnant or dead. Plus, you need a Masters Degree in Statistical Analysis to figure out the fare structure.

Another alternative is the bus, but you're likely get stuck in a jam. Here, from your lofty perch, you can witness the frustrated weaving of parents driving a few hundred yards to school. In a few isolated places there are bus lanes, but these are clogged by taxis, delivery drivers and squashed cyclists. Not everywhere has space for a bus lane. Local roads were designed for horse and cart so the only way to create bus lanes would be to make the whole of northern England a one-way system.

The tram network is a fairly recent innovation, installed at no little expense. These are not the characterful, clattering beasts of yesteryear, the likes of which trundled up and down the prom at Blackpool, umbilicals flashing blue as they take nourishment from overhead cables. No, modern trams are evil-looking worms that run on tracks where roads used to be.

But it appears that they are eco-friendly. I read that an estimated 70% of a Metrolink tram's power is provided by wind or solar/photovoltaic sources. This means that the back three carriages have to hope there isn't a diesel shortage. Locally, trams have proved a low-speed, moderate cost means of getting out of Rochdale to go and shop somewhere else, largely because the main shopping streets of my day now look like East Berlin after a particularly determined bombing raid.

It's becoming a world of techno-socialism where jobs for machines are guaranteed and people's unemployment benefit is paid for by parking fines. Budgetary pressures mean that the only people who can maintain their standard of living are politicians who vote themselves inflation-busting pay hikes for the privilege of making the lives of ordinary mortals considerably more miserable. Of course, in our democracy we can always vote them out but what will happen when it becomes a technocracy, when we will be 'managed' by machines? We're on the way already with lawn mowers and vacuum cleaners that are wholly independent (after you've switched them on). They are quite happy bouncing between electronic boundaries. Next step is to make them human-shaped and we'll have an army of electronic domestic technicians. That'll be my wife's friend out of a job to start with.

The human heart and fresh air will become redundant as A.I. (Artificial Intelligence) humanoids take over completely. If we need to complain about our robot (Plastic Pat) because she is leaving eggy smears on the side-plates, our fully automated local authority complaints department won't be a big help. We'll press this, press that and be told by a human-shaped vacuum cleaner that our call is irrelevant and we are welcome to use the Internet to complain about their website that doesn't work.

I'm contemplating all this when, through our plastic front door, a blizzard of leaflets arrives advertising grants for solar power in a land where the sun don't shine. Water, however, a commodity that reliably arrives by the reservoir-full, gets increasingly expensive. When I were a lad we used to shower with a friend or lob a brick in the cistern, now every time we flush the bog a Utilities shareholder puts away another few quid for their Florida trip.

As I gaze out of the window wondering how I can harness the sun's power without investing fifteen thousand, a group of marauding 'hoodlums' hustles past, hoodies up, engulfed in a cloud of sweet-smelling fog. They are unchecked because our pair of Special Constables, who have to patrol three hundred thousand square miles of northern England on foot, are bogged down with paperwork.

Yes, one thing that has definitely changed for the worse is 'respect.' In many areas really, but not least on the roads. People rarely seem to own up to a mistake; it's the 'never admit liability' syndrome where, even is somebody is in the wrong, they go on the attack in an effort to transfer the blame.

I came across a boy of about twelve kicking the hell out of a bed of crocuses. I asked him to stop and was given a disgusting volley of abuse before he zoomed off on an electric scooter. Willfully destroying flowers, how moronic is that? Was I that bad as a youngster? Don't answer! I'm sure there are acts of kindness and plenty of good deeds. It just seems as if they are being somewhat swamped by the scruffy aspects of modern life.

Rochdale is a place much changed, some of it improved. My wife and I arranged to meet daughter and grandchildren (3 yrs, and 10 months) at Rochdale library - that is no longer a library. Currently called Touchstones, it is a museum, art gallery, local studies centre and café and has had good write-ups. We wanted to give the three-year-old a taste of his heritage and I wanted a baked potato. Sadly, it is not the most accessible place. Our daughter was encumbered with prams and nappies so needed a relatively local parking spot. Unfortunately, the visit was cancelled because she couldn't find one – except for half a dozen empty disabled bays right outside. My wife and I were inside studying the menu so were no help at all. There is a drop-off space right outside, but that would have meant dumping children, plus a mountain of child accessories, on the pavement while she went to find a parking space - and goodness knows where that might have been. No, instead, we went to a local hotel 'of some maturity' up on a hill. There was plenty of parking because it looked like the place had been abandoned. But no, we had a quick coffee in the resident's lounge and went home.

My wife and I actually did visit Touchstones subsequently and I have to say it is (largely) very impressive. Because we aren't officially disabled, we had to walk some distance to get to it, but it was worth the effort. The cafe was being patronised by mainly retired folks out for a tasty, sensibly priced (cheap) lunch, in addition to one very prosperous-looking lady tapping away feverishly on a laptop. A council employee, possibly, scheming ways to fleece more money from local taxpayers. The grub was good, as was the museum of local history which reminded us that this area (industrial Lancashire) used to be at the very heart of the world's wealth – although it can be argued with the benefit of slave-like employment practices. Nevertheless, we used to produce textile by the multi-tonne in monstrous, mille-feuille factories. That pleasant little French description has a nice ring, doesn't it? It somewhat glosses over the multi-floor misery endured by the grafters within. Most factories are gone and we now produce far less of, er, anything.

The art gallery was less to our taste, however. In our opinion, and to use the local vernacular, this particular exhibition was 'a waste of space' - literally. One room, the approximate size of a gymnasium, housed about a dozen foot-square paintings daubed by an artist of modest talent. The pictures were spread so sparingly round the walls that we needed one of the aforementioned buses to join the dots. I realize that exhibitions are put together by arty types for the benefit of arty types but suspect that normal human beings find the whole thing rather minimalist. This is Lancashire, after all, where a guinea is expected for a pound. For those who don't remember pre-decimal days, a guinea was a quarter ounce of West African gold worth twenty-one shillings (where one pound was twenty shillings). Interestingly, a guinea is also a kick to the lower leg and a tasty bird.

As a footnote, my wife worked at the art gallery for a spell. She was tasked with hanging a display 'created' by a London artist. The concoction was made up of twenty-four medical X-rays to be hung in a sequential grid. They didn't make up a full body – nothing so sensible, no; they were just a random assortment of parts of the body, some fractured. They were not numbered, so what could go wrong? My wife duly risked life and limb up and down a set of steps and displayed the masterpiece, only to be told by the artist, when he finally arrived, that she'd hung it all upside down. Who the hell would have noticed is anyone's guess, but my wife's career as art gallery operative came to a grinding halt a short time later. The tragedy is that there is a cellar full of real paintings, some very accomplished stuff apparently, so one has to question the decision to exhibit a dozen mediocre, tiddly paintings of dubious provenance or a selection of fractured feet.

The point of this is that our rather nice library is no longer in the rather nice library building. Intrigued, I search the Internet for Rochdale library. It tells me that it's on Smith Street but I don't know where that is. A photograph shows it to be one module within a much larger collection of modern glass/concrete modules. How can the blockhead who designed this new building possibly consider it more aesthetically pleasing than the wonderful, intricate stone-built original? I took to the Internet and clicked on the Rochdale Library website link and ... 'Server Error. 404 – File or Directory Not Found.' If I'd had a couple of months to spare I could have phoned the local authority customer services department, but I didn't ... so I didn't.

The lost library somehow illustrates life today, particularly to an ageing dunce like me with little sense of direction. Things have changed, seemingly at random, in an effort to make life more streamlined – but it hasn't. What it's done is confuse dinosaurs like me who like it simple.

On a positive note, the centre of town actually looks very impressive after recent renovations. The River Roch used to flow beneath the esplanade, but it's been uncovered. Released from its dingy course, it flows below street level, slightly sinister. Just as the River Styx formed the boundary between Earth (Gaia) and the underworld, so the River Roch separates the Bingo Hall from The NatWest Bank across the square. It's wonderful actually, a credit to the planners. As a bonus, when I visit my bank I can see a fascinating assortment of plastic bags and discarded underwear drift towards the west.

About a third of the Town Hall car park is now pedestrianised and they've put up a lovely statue to Gracie Fields. Proud of her we are, too, though she left for the Mediterranean as soon as funds allowed. 'Wish me luck as you wave me goodbye ...' Sadly, at least whenever I visit, there are so few people about it looks like there's been an anthrax alert.

Anyone returning, like me, to the area after a sabbatical and unaware of 'municipal manipulations,' will find the layout altered. Anyone looking for a swim will find instead a German supermarket. I have fond memories, except perhaps of being leered at by the lecherous old git who posed as a lifeguard in the old swimming baths. Unless my memory is playing tricks, there used to be an iron security grill over the entrance. Back then, the building's interior looked like a 19th century lunatic asylum with floor to ceiling, nearly-white tiles and institutional lighting. There was an overpowering smell of disinfectant and freezing winds whistled through bleak passages (bit like my school, actually). But apart from the dodgy lifeguard it was somehow all rather comforting, and local folks who'd just done a few lengths in their wool-knit swimsuits could get a slice of buttered toast and a beaker of Horlicks in the caff. Those were the days when, aged 10, I could get the bus from Littleborough to Rochdale with little fear of being trafficked.

I need to close for now. Another ream of leaflets has just dropped onto the doormat and I need to decide which new bathroom suite not to buy.

Chat in a Northern Park

2016

Why the heck is everybody so chatty? Don't they know there's a recession on? Or if there's isn't, we're probably about to have one. In the North of England, roughly in the centre of the British Isles, everyone speaks – well not everyone, but most. I have the uncharitable belief that people only converse to find someone who is even more miserable than they are. There is often a bout of verbal jousting, a sort of conversational foreplay, to discover who has the direst woes. People are looking for serious health issues or financial meltdown. Even a broken bicycle would cheer them up, or a leaking radiator. They soon move on when you tell them you're doing fine, thank you. They become wary of anyone who doesn't have at least one malady and slope off to find someone who is prepared to tell the truth.

A dog walk round the park can take nearly an hour (and it's only a few hundred yards), not because I've got knackered hips and there are a couple of hills; no, it's folk wanting to talk, even if it's chucking it down. In the space of half an hour the other morning I'd learned from two total strangers that one bloke's son was having marital difficulties in Sydney, Australia - 'He's made his bed ...' – and a woman's washing machine was on the blink. 'My Gran managed perfectly well with a slab of stone and mangle,' she tells me. 'Eh, those were the days.' I pointed out that if she'd been using a slab and a mangle she probably wouldn't have had a break down. She looked at me expectantly, hoping I would tell her that one of my appliances was on the blink.

You see, people want you to agree with them. They want to feel a problem shared. If you tell them your washing machine has worked perfectly for a decade, they don't like it. You're just showing off. It's better to lie and say you just had a flood. That way lies not antagonism but empathy and the chance of a lasting relationship.

If there's a difficult pause, the way to get things back on track is to change direction. Surprise them by offering up something wacky. It's conversational kill or cure. You'll either part company quickly and get home to your porridge or you can linger under the trees and have a meaningful discussion about, for example, why camels don't get sunburn.

Dogs are a great bringer-together of people. I tend to remember the dog's name rather than the owner. Dog-related conversation is usually pleasant, unless you're being attacked. We generally find something nice to say. Even if the dog looks a bit irregular, we compliment the owner on the colouring. To dive in and ask, for example, 'What's wrong with it then?' is a sure way to lose friends in dog circles. Yes, I enjoy dog chats, particularly on the odd occasion the sun shines in the Pennine north.

Though I do get wrapped up in extensive discussions from time to time, I like the brief, snappy conversation during my park walks. Actually, I'm better with a brief conversation. I can usually come up with something witty or daft. It's when the chat goes on for a bit that my shortcomings begin to surface. I'm not that widely travelled or worldly experienced but I've done enough to be able to talk a little about most things – at least join in without looking like a half-wit.

Sometimes you come across a conversational 'one-tracker,' the person who only has one thing to talk about. People get a bee in their bonnet about something and want to gush forth - the National Health Service or dog poo are two likely subjects. You can see them coming; they have that manic look in their eye and you instinctively know they have some burdensome issue they want to offload. It's open-air community counseling, really, as we stand there and absorb other people's woes. It's the Northern English version of the gatherings of elderly folk doing Tai Chi in a Tokyo park. My Dutch mate is a one-tracker. All he wants to talk about is cars, and a particular model of Japanese sports car at that. Whenever the conversation looks like drifting away he drags it back. 'Look at that lovely apple blossom,' I would say. 'Yes, I parked under a tree like that in the south of France once. I was on a driving holiday ...'

There's only so much I can expound on Japanese sports cars, and a lot of that revolves about how I can't afford one. But undeterred he rambles on about how he's just got the latest halogen headlights - meanwhile I drift off somewhere deep inside my dim grey matter, wondering if my car door will open because some lout kicked it while I was doing my weekly £3 shop in a German supermarket.

The formal park in which I converse was laid down by the wealthy, benevolent Newall family in Victorian times. They also built factories where people got smeared with grease for 60 hours a week before grabbing a few minutes watching the brass band play in the brass band stand in our park. The factories are largely gone but the skeletal band stand remains, surrounded by meandering paths, rhododendrons and manicured lawns - or is it grass? When does grass become a lawn, or vice versa? I must seek opinion on my next walk - someone will know. Unless it's my Dutch mate: 'Yes, I once stopped for a picnic next to a lawn. I was on a driving tour of Germany in my sports car with the new headlamps and ...'

By night the youth of the town compete to determine who can throw a fast food carton the furthest so, particularly on Sunday mornings, there is a bit of litter about. The dog enjoys the smells. On one occasion he emerged from the bushes looking particularly pleased with himself with a full burger bun in his mouth. It looked like a set of comedy lips. Yes, me and my fellow walkers tread a messy, Sabbath-day path. (Revolting, rotting rubbish – there you are, a litteration!). Fortunately, there are park staff in high-vis jackets who trundle around on a mini tractors and soon return the park to its ornamental splendour. It's the circle of life, really. Someone throws something on the floor, someone else picks it up.

The canal runs through our little town. The Rochdale canal. Now, as discussed, anything associated with Rochdale needs a good PR team to sell it, but the canal around Littleborough is looked after and enhanced by local volunteers. Village folk who have a real pride in the area. I joined them a couple of times. I've been too busy recently but I'll try and get back again. I worked alongside a chap chopping back some bushes along the tow path so locals and visitors could have a walk without getting an eye poked out by a stray branch. It turns out that he is the brother of the bloke who lives next door to the little house we bought as an investment. Investment, huh! It's the only house outside

Damascus that has gone down in value over the past 6 months – so probably a good topic of conversation on a dog walk and empathy with someone who's oven has just exploded!

My tree-chopping association typifies another aspect of village life, even a large one like ours (village, not tree). Everybody knows everybody; if not directly, at least once removed. My wife's mate has a large extended family and it appears that everybody is married to one of her relatives. Or separated from.

It seems that the more you get to know someone the less you know about them. We've been away for 25 years but almost every time my wife ventures out she encounters someone with whom she was at school. Despite physical 'developments,' they recognize one another instantly and another friendship is rekindled. The very responsible practice nurse at the doctors' surgery is the daughter of one of Jan's school pals. Last seen scrabbling around the local park in a shell suit, she's now a sensible grown-up with whom local folk trust their health and who will spawn the next generation – or has already started, I'm not sure. I was too polite to ask – particularly as I was wearing an over-tight blood-pressure bandage and she was waving a needle around.

While we've been away the village has been thriving and regenerating, nurtured by these friendly folk in the Pennines. There is a whole new group with whom we can discuss camels and kitchen appliances on our walks in the park – and it's great.

Can you see? After a difficult, uncertain start, I'm already more optimistic.

My wife was historically more involved with the village than me. I was sent away to school. This meant I largely lost touch with all my young friends. We went our separate ways and I regretted not having a bosom to come home to - if you get my meaning. But even I can see that some things haven't changed intrinsically. The physical structure is similar, even if more houses have been built to bloat it. Even one or two shops have the same name as 25 years ago. One in fact has the same till! It's the takeaway I used to frequent when fatty food of uncertain origin was not deemed to be life-threatening. Goodness knows why I remember the till, but I do, and commented on the fact to the proprietor who, it transpires, was a junior member of staff during my day. He's now the boss and shovelling cash into his ancient machinery. He's made a lasting success of his business, certainly not a conversation topic in the park. The hacked-off elephant's leg tastes just as good and the boss is still an amiable, chatty soul. At least some things haven't changed.

Above the village looms Blackstone Edge, a section of Pennine moorland. A road snakes over the top towards Yorkshire, a road only taken out of necessity by the people of our village. Lancashire folk would rather stay in Lancashire (unless they've had a particularly unsatisfactory walk in the park and feel the need to re-centre). They would also prefer that Yorkshire folk remain on their side of the hill. Despite having things in common, like Indian takeaways and no more mills, the skirmishes of the Roses continue in a friendly banter sort of way.

Having spent some time down south (England, not Africa) I know where I would rather be. 'Down there' it's not easy to engage someone in conversation and if you do there is too much one-upmanship. I often felt to be speaking with someone's husk, as if the person within needed to be protected by a materialistic veneer. In the north it's often the opposite as people charge right in with their direst vulnerability – and usually there is sincere sympathy and no nonsense advice in return.

Though I can sense a shift. People appear to have more disposable income, more chattels. Or is it merely an illusion because goods are more readily available on credit? Granny used to save up to buy a new yard brush, nowadays we buy one 'over twelve months' and have it delivered next day - or pay someone else to sweep up. Also skewing my perspective is an influx of wealthy people who have arrived to fill the ever-expanding stock of pricey houses.

We talk and talk, then text and message via electronic device these days. In fact, couples have been known to text each other from within their own house. Children are summoned for supper via email from the kitchen, the nerve-centre of domestic communication. A photo of a sausage is instagrammed to Dad in his shed - tea is ready. But thankfully the art of chat is not dead. Just take a walk round the park with a dog. Sure, there are regulars who update you on misbehaving appliances, but you may also come across someone new. A lurker in the bushes who could suddenly pop out and start a conversation about the unlikeliest subject.

Occasionally something crops up that I could have done without. For example, this tale relates to a man I know only vaguely. He's someone I occasionally catch in the beam of my head torch in the early morning. The other day I asked how he was. 'Not so good actually,' he replies, 'I've a nasty abscess low down to the rear. Mighty uncomfortable it is. Having a right old job with the number twos.'

'Oh dear.'

A couple of days later I see him again and inquire of his difficulties.

'Still bad, but I think it's slightly better.' Then, with a straight face, 'There's light at the end of the tunnel.'

What an image that is to take home for breakfast!

One thing I never saw many years ago was a deer. But I came across one the other day. It was just standing near the football fields where the dog was having a romp. It had the casual air of a deer who has escaped the cull on a highland estate and migrated south. It appeared relaxed in the knowledge that folk who bemoan their dodgy ovens are unlikely to be armed with a rifle. It was standing patiently on the touchline, awaiting an invitation to join in with the locals – much like us, really.

Water and Chips

2017

Water and chips attract visitors, particularly when the sleet abates. Such is the case at Hollingworth Lake on the outskirts of Littleborough. When I was a lad it was just a lake but nowadays it's a tourist trap – a place for townies to get some fresh air and devour heart-stopping grub. Consequently, when the sun shines it's busy – much busier than I remember. It turns out that what we now have is a revival. Built as a feeder for the Rochdale Canal, Hollingworth Lake was actually developed as a tourist resort in the 1860s. At the height of its popularity, helped by the arrival of the nearby railway, the lake boasted three lake steamers and a lifeboat. Visitors flocked from Manchester, Bradford and Leeds. Here, look at this! It was written in Davenport's guide in Victorian times:

> *"As you step on the embankment, which is considerable and scarcely looks artificial, the broad expanse of water at once presents itself to your vision. Your first feeling on beholding it is that of astonishment that so vast a basin, lying in that cup of hills, should not have become known to you before. ... You will see Blackstone Edge to the east,*

> *towering above its fellows, and preaching from its rocky*
> *pulpit sermons to the solitude around."*

And I had the temerity to think it was just a lake. I suppose we have to bear in mind that in the lake's early days, most people spent twenty-three hours a day dodging flying shuttles in the mill. Everybody would have been exhausted and likely deaf, so appreciation of the lake and pretty Pennine hills would have held even more allure. It's now in its second heyday (if you can have more than one heyday) which started when it became an official Country Park back in 1974. Visitors are welcoming of, in ascending order of 'attractiveness', amusement arcade, chippies, restaurants, pubs, the lake, a wildlife conservation area and the surrounding beauty. These days cars bring visitors and, when the sun shines, surrounding roads get a bit clogged - but the point is that we have something worth visiting and we should be proud of that.

Some things are faster, like the dash for the open surgery during a snuffle epidemic. Some things are slower, like buses trapped on the A58, a clotted artery between Littleborough and Rochdale – basically a long, thin car park. Some things are more frustrating, like trying to find a village-centre parking spot or traversing a street where those who have been unable to find a designated parking space (or can't be bothered to walk a few yards) abandon expensive vehicles wherever they feel like it.

But reassuringly some things trundle on as before in the name of fun, good causes or social networking. These nuggets (referred to in previous pages) have always been there, it's just that they are rather harder to find these days.

The Townswomen's Guild (TG) still dispenses beverage and biscuit with determination and coiffured diligence, these days with a fun, pink tinge to the hairdos. You can still get a good pint of ale - though one brew in particular is proving a bit dangerous. It's offered by a local establishment that brews its own beers, including a strong lager at about 8%. According to a friend, it's the local equivalent of poteen (a lethal Irish moonshine). My mate (only) had four pints but staggered home. Disturbingly, as the brew continued to mature, he begun to have hallucinations and spent most of the night wide awake, fending off imaginary invaders. I worked with him the following day and he had that thousand-yard stare, as if he'd just survived a particularly nasty battle.

The opportunity for a good meal has increased. At least two new eateries have recently opened their doors and have great reviews on the local discussion pages (where you get found out pretty quickly if you put a foot wrong). You can also walk the canal towpath or trek in the hills.

U3A (University of the Third Age) is a relatively new institution where folks of a certain age can learn new skills and participate in group activities. One can learn Latin or have a bash at the ukulele perhaps. The local branch is only a couple of years old but, so popular has it proved, it has nearly outgrown it's 100+ meeting room.

Other things seem to have disappeared into the mists. When was the last time you saw a hopscotch grid? Been a while, I bet, and there are probably sound explanations why. Firstly, these days youngsters can play virtual hopscotch, prodding away with lightening-fast fingers from the comfort of an unmade bed in mission control. If they did venture outside they'd likely be arrested for chalking the pavement - after washing off dog leftovers. But before all that, they'd need to find a level bit. Despite personal injury lawyers' best efforts the pavements are maintained worse than the roads. Any child under four feet tall is in danger of hopping straight down a pot-hole, never to be seen again. They would join the ghosts of their forebears deep underground, hacking away at a coal seam. Friends would record another's demise on a gadget, post it on Facebook and share a giggle. What's not to like? Additional hazards are taxis parked on the footpaths and 4x4s passing at such speed that youngsters are likely to be sucked off the pavement by a vortex. No, these days it's safer to watch telly.

There is a glimmer of light. Kids play football on the pitches near our house, egged on by eager parents. They're certainly learning from their professional counterparts, judging by the pile of discarded water bottles strewn about after the weekend. But it's great to see youngsters charging about at all, free of electronic comfort blankets for a while. Mind you, they're a pitch down on yesteryear because one has been turned (expensively) into a swamp. It's actually part of a flood-alleviation scheme where a pitch was excavated to create a six-feet-deep pan. Although it prevents people's gardens flooding half a mile up the hill, it now floods a former football pitch instead. Looking optimistically there could be wildlife/twitcher potential here? Cranes, razor bills and egrets could break their journey between Blackburn and Huddersfield attracted by this new wonder-wetland. *Townhouse Road Wildlife Swamp* - has a ring to it, I feel.

Local services are rather hit and miss. At the end of our avenue there was a streetlight in danger of becoming overwhelmed by rampant foliage. The light failed, so one of our neighbours phoned the utility company and the light was repaired within a few hours. Spurred on by this success he called the council to have the trees trimmed back so the light could operate at maximum efficiency and illuminate the car park and adjacent swamp. 'Certainly,' said the polite official, 'we'll put you on the waiting list.' 'Wonderful!' replied our neighbour, delighted by the council's positive response. 'How soon do you think you'll be able to get here?' 'Let me check. Er.... the waiting list is currently four years.'

When we bought our little house it had seven wheelie bins – seven! As far as I'm aware, it was the only domicile in town where the bins were worth more than the house. One was pinched and I gave another away (to someone else who'd had one pinched) so we're now down to manageable proportions - plus the waste food bin, of course. Gone are the days when one metal bin was humped into a fetid truck by operatives with Herculean strength. These days things are generally more disposable – like fridges and televisions and other detritus that all too often ends up in country lanes. The cost of disposal is the problem - it's easier to open your van's back doors on a slight incline than pay to go to the tip.

In Holland, where we lived for a spell, they are VERY strict on waste disposal. You drive up to the tip, your car is weighed and you're charged on both the weight and recyclability of what you're dumping. For wood you pay just by weight. Old insulation is expensive, not heavy by weight, but very heavy by tariff. The policing is diligent and fines hefty for those breaking the rules. Holland is flat and the majority of people live in the south west of the country, a bit like a snooker table with a leg missing. But it's a very clean country, almost to the point of sterility. Where we are now in the Pennine foothills is rather more ramshackle and hilly. I prefer that, actually.

Littleborough is a large village and inflating. It's a town to all intents and purposes; in fact, some say it's a town by right.

We could really do with a road-widening scheme to help us get in and out. Sadly, that's unlikely because it would mean the compulsory purchase of a couple of thousand road-side houses, a ruck of shops and the odd church.

Littleborough's high street shops are all occupied and a good mix they are, too. Yes there's one popular 'budget' shop (where you can pick up a variant of a well-known toothpaste with Cyrillic writing on it) but also quality establishments such as a bakers, a deli, and two butchers. There are a couple of 'designer' clothes shops too - I'm told that at least one Coronation Street star visits. Is that a recommendation?

Since my youth, we're down one gents' outfitters, a green-grocers and a fishmongers, largely due to the influence of supermarkets. Banks are a bit thin on the ground too. There were at least two; now it's online or Rochdale. I have a frustrating visit to the HSBC in Rochdale in the next chapter.

Still on a shopping theme, one thing that has changed radically is the exponential rise in consumer goods designed to make us more anti-social. TVs, fancy phones and portable entertainment gadgets all enable us to inhabit a virtual world where personal contact is rendered virtually unnecessary. The authorities have considerately removed our iconic red post boxes so game-players watching a 'Kardashian video' while walking the streets don't crash into a red pillar. We scrimp, save or borrow to buy the biggest, fanciest accessories so we can watch and listen to an ever-increasing back catalogue of drivel in splendid isolation.

A friend of ours came to dinner the other night and he was wearing a 'smartwatch.' It was a monster and permanently illuminated (presumably so people have to ask about it). He dangled his hand down the side of the chair and twitched his wrist, trying to draw my attention to 'Big Ben', so I'd have to ask about it. When he showed signs of repetitive strain injury, I eventually asked him. A marvellous piece of kit it turned out to be. It had GPS technology (global positioning satellite) which tells you, at the press of a button, whether you are in the kitchen or the lounge. Plus, not only will it warn you that your heartbeat is reaching danger levels while walking to the chippy, it also tells you if it's raining. I'd not come across one before so did a little research. Apparently you can search the Internet and 'get important notifications sent straight to your wrist' (!!?). Apparently you can pay for your groceries without getting your wallet out. I can see me having all sorts of problems with that!

It's not only the capital cost of these things, it's the ongoing subscriptions. Well over a thousand pounds a year – more in many cases (considerably less in ours). That's very nearly a train ticket to Cornwall, for goodness sake. I worked at a house recently and they had four TVs, all better than ours – and ours isn't bad. Smart is the 'in' word, isn't it?

Years ago there was no broadband, mobile phones, Sky, Netflix or Amazon Prime. These are all additional expenses we have to bear today - or not, if funds don't run to it. Plus, anything I really want to watch on TV is subscription only – sport mainly. Though I realize that balls are not everyone's cup of tea, it's something that I would have to pay for if I was so inclined (or adequately solvent). My alternative is watching a bunch of talentless dipsticks arguing over the (staged) cost of antiques or overblown cookery experts using ingredients that health experts on another programme tell us will kill us. For those on and around the minimum wage, and there are plenty of them, you have to work for the thick end of a month to pay for your basic extra subscriptions. There's not much smart about that as far as I can see.

So what's improved in the last twenty years? Well, the availability of stuff perhaps. Shopping is easier (if you can get there) with the advent of more competition and choice of goods. Our German friends have shaken the traditional outlets out of any complacency they may have had. We can now buy buffalo and reindeer or procure fruit and exotic veggies year round. And of course you can shop online. Without doubt there are savings to be made compared to the high street but it's a bit too easy to surf on your gadget and end up buying what normally would only have been a 'possible.' However, thanks to the rise in courier companies, it's easy (too easy?) to return goods. I've heard that people buy an article of clothing, wear it once, then send it back. Wouldn't have happened in the gentleman's outfitters of times past. I remember Vernon Haigh on Church Street, a wonderful, traditional emporium. To this day I can recall the smell of leather and marvel that Mr Haigh could find things so quickly among the hundreds of wooden drawers. I can only imagine his response if I'd taken back a jacket with a dollop of ketchup on it.

My brother-in-law's eyes were failing, so he requested a radio to listen to sport. I suggested a DAB type. Now whether that was good advice or not is open to question but I went to buy him one from a major electronics retailer (one that you might encounter at an Indian Restaurant, perhaps?!). They had a fair number of models in stock, a few of which were in our price range, so I asked for a demonstration. Every radio sat there and hissed, except one, and that was playing Punjabi music. (I suspected it was a recording!) I pointed out to the (very helpful) assistant that this wasn't overly promising. 'They don't work very well inside this building,' she said. 'It's the roof, I think.'

'Oh,' I replied, 'my brother-in-law has a roof. Will he have to sit in his back yard to listen to his radio?' Just in case, I paid a few quid extra and bought a water-resistant model - from the supermarket next door!

The best things are still free. Fresh air hereabouts, or the innocent smiles and sparkly eyes of our grandsons (unless they are teething or have the shits, in which case they are best left alone). Seeing my brother-in-law chuckle (while sitting outside in the drizzle listening to his new radio) is a joy after the hand he's been dealt. We still have pockets of snowdrops and daffodils which haven't been buried under concrete and brick. Cherry blossom still dazzles in our park and we're fighting the designer dog poo battle with determination on many fronts (or rears). Yes, the local park is a gem. There are many walkers and we see kiddies playing in the play area, which is now also a place of fun and intrigue for our grandchildren. It's all kept clean and tidy largely by our lady park-keeper who does a fabulous job charging about in her high-vis gear. Cath (or is it Kath?), we salute you, and thank you.

The park was originally the private garden of Hare Hill House, home to a wealthy local businessman in times gone by. The house is being restored by volunteers for the benefit of the community and was snatched from the clutches of the local council, who wanted to turn it into flats (or apartments - they would have been a bit posh to call flats). My wife and I occasionally volunteer at social functions at the house - she as a waitress/hostess where she banters with guests. She's a bit of a character, actually, and at the most recent function wore a large pair of butterfly wings and coloured her hair green with chalk paint in deference to St. Patrick, whose birthday we were all using as an excuse to get sozzled. I help out on the bar (which is a bit like tethering a camel in an oasis). The other volunteers are a nice bunch from a variety of backgrounds with a varied selection of skills, some of them relevant. But we all have something in common – doing something for nothing for the benefit of the village. That is not meant to sound pompous or self-righteous; it's fun, with nice people. I think we all get a cozy feeling when a function goes well. We're reminded that we need to keep at it because at the Irish function rainwater dripped into a couple of buckets behind the bar, a symptom of the knackered roof. I have to be clear here, I only help out occasionally, other volunteers are regulars and it's thanks to them that we have a community house where local folk can have some fun.

You see, it takes time to come to terms with all the frustrating stuff, but when you do there are gems. Overall, we're getting there. My problem is that I was basing 'now' on 'then' and I can't do that – things are not the same, never will be, however much I wish it. We have to adapt and live today. I bumped into a friend with whom I used to play cricket and golf. He now goes crown-green bowling. 'Come along,' he says. 'It's fun. We generally play for an hour or so then go for a pint.' Now that sounds more like it. Dawn, it appears, is breaking.

All-Purpose SUV

2018

I don't know much about cars but in the last quarter-century there has been an exponential increase in automotive acronyms. For example, MDPV (Medium Duty Passenger Vehicle) which may have gHCCI (Gasoline Homogeneous Charge Compression Ignition) – neither of which I have. Is the second one a selling point? Would you walk into a showroom and request a car with gHCCI? No.

My Morris 1300 didn't have any acronyms but you did see the occasional 'L' (Luxury, I think, which the Morris wasn't!). I asked my wife if she remembered what 'L' stood for. 'Learner', she said, which I thought was quite good. You saw the occasional TC or PI (twin carb or petrol injection) or Vanden Plas for the posh ones, but nothing like the confusing hieroglyphics of today.

What I actually have is an auto, FWD, PAS, SSW, TP, KOW (automatic, front-wheel drive, power assisted steering, single steering wheel, twin pedal, knackered old wreck – with AC that doesn't work). Basically, it can all be nut-shelled into my SUV – Scabby, Uninspiring Vauxhall. In the three years we've been back I've been renovating houses using the SUV as a works van. Consequently, as I write, my trusty steed is almost completely buggered. But not quite; it rattles on doggedly.

I regularly drive it to the Builders Merchants, a round trip of about six miles. Outbound I'm empty and my vehicle is skittish. It performs like a featherweight ballerina, dancing from pothole to pothole. On the return trip I'm usually laden, sometimes heavily, with timber, cement and plasterboard which make my dear old motor's undercarriage groan. These materials are required to make a hash of my latest project. Actually, the outbound trip is not always empty because I make a diversion to the local tip. More often than not I'm depositing low-mileage raw materials into a large bin due to another cock-up, materials that frankly deserve a better fate.

This is not wholly about my car's shortcomings, it's partly a reflection on what's going on in the world's subconscious. As we drive from A to B we are cocooned in our vehicles in a safe, soundproofed haven, isolated from reality, oblivious to the ire and angst of the world-weary masses beyond our isolated luxury. To be honest you can't associate my SUV with luxury travel, unless you compare it to the lass I've just zoomed past. She's battling along in the drizzle on her not-new bike.

Let's pause for a moment to think about what's going on outside. If we could read people's thoughts perhaps we might be more empathetic? To the cycling lass for example who's thinking, 'What have I done to deserve this?' Other road users are rudely dismissive of her vulnerability. Her commute is rotten preparation for her working day, particularly if her job entails smiling and grovelling to customers for eight hours. The world around us must be full of thoughts, a miasma of random ideas, wasted and unfulfilled as they drift away into the damp Pennine morning, leeching into the air like smoke from a damp bonfire.

Those less fortunate than me (and there are not many) watch

as I glide by in my SUV. Back in the mists of time Prometheus was probably full of optimism when he created mankind, generously donating the fire he stole from Mount Olympus to help us on our way. Has evolution gone quite the way he anticipated during the intervening aeons? Not sure, but quite what he would have made of the bloke at the bus stop peering out from the depths of a menacing white smog is anyone's guess. It's actually the exhaust from his vaping machine to which he's taken in an effort to get fit. He glares at me with snakey, steam-filled eyes and I know what he'll be thinking: 'Lucky bastard. There he goes, lording it in his fancy motor, nose in the air. Hope you break down, you prick, then we'll see just how smug you are.' He's actually still in the same bus stop two and a half hours later when I return. Either that particular bus route has been discontinued or he is so well hidden in his cloud that the bus driver failed to spot him.

And he's mistaken. My nose is in the air because I have to peer over a parabolic smear on the windscreen where a bluebottle got mashed under the windscreen wiper. Meanwhile I'm being overtaken by one of those annoying characters in a big 4 x 4 - 'I'll just piss everybody off' - as he sneaks down the outside lane hoping to make up a couple of car lengths.

I need fuel. The lady in the petrol station is politeness personified. (Petrol note, not diesel - mine is an environmentally neutral SUV, at least till the year 2030.) Poor lady hasn't got time to think due to the never-ending stream of vehicles pulling in out of the permanent traffic jam. Smiling (or at least appearing to be pleasant) is a skill that must be conquered by those in service jobs. Frustrated as she must be by the repetitive nature of her work she shows remarkable self-control. People are impatient these days and always desperate to re-join life's traffic jam. Customer impatience is reflected in stilted conversations ending, with luck, with a terse 'thank you.' But the lady in the petrol station has to treat everyone with equal respect - which must be a real test at times. It takes seventeen muscles to form a smile but only three or four to thump someone in the face, so she shows admirable restraint.

I always try and make a conscious effort to be pleasant, try and spark up a conversation, however brief. My efforts don't always break the ice. I asked a chap in the DIY the other day what measures he was taking to treat his facial spots. An innocent enough question, you would have thought, which didn't deserve the side-of-the-mouth mutterings I received in response. People rarely have much time to chat these days - unless they're selling you something. I'd only asked because I have developed facial dermatitis. This a new one for me, adding to the growing list of late-middle-age irregularities. Blotchy, flaky stuff has suddenly erupted on my face and forehead. I put it down to stress and too little red wine, one of which I can address forthwith. The doc was less sure and prescribed me something that would get me a ban if I was an elite athlete. I'm going to persist with the wine in case the doc is mistaken. This wasn't my regular doctor - who is a man and, as such, someone more likely to understand the appalling habits of a fellow male. No, this one was a lady who likely thought that I treated my body less as a temple than a sewage treatment plant. With some justification perhaps.

Years ago, when I was more image conscious, I remember once having an ache in a private area. Very much a male problem, I booked to see my doctor, a man of middle years with whom I banter unrestrainedly. I walked into the surgery to find a girl, only about three hours out of junior school, acting as locum. My examination was a guarded affair on both sides. She knew I was 'flustered' so she tried to put me at ease with a constant stream of chatter. She started, 'Look out, cold hands' and finished with a big grin and 'Nothing of consequence down there.' That really helped, I can tell you.

I pass a lollipop lady then a chap on a ride-on mower trimming the grass on the central reservation. Both wear yellow uniforms. Actually 'uniforms' is pushing it a bit, outfits more like, but both are taking their life in their hands working so close to us motorists. They are highly visible but it only takes one plonker on a mobile phone to cause carnage. It's dangerous work despite the fact they both have weapons; one a threatening lollipop, the other a high-speed chopper.

Closing in on the Builders Merchant's, I get held up by a bin wagon. Blue ones today, relieving us of our surplus cardboard which will be burned to keep the council offices at a pleasant seventy degrees. The operatives also wear yellow - public servant yellow. Sure, they are all highly visible, but the local council is highlighting where our tax pounds are being spent. These operatives are the council's public face and because they stand out it feels as if there are more of them than there actually are. In fact, the remaining 99% of council employees, the ones who collect the taxes or refuse planning permissions or design automated telephone systems to tell us the library has closed, all wear mufti. The invisible hoards are well hidden behind smoked glass and discontinued phone lines.

As I head into town I pass through a predominantly Asian area where thoughts and cultures collide. I've seen an extraordinary change during my lifetime. There are no-go areas, not because of danger but because there seems to be little common ground between the incomers and indigenous. I'm not referring to fanatics here; there are fanatics in every culture. No, I'm talking about ordinary everyday folk who just want to live. The problem is that there are so many different backgrounds, histories and cultures that there just doesn't seem to be enough common ground. Things seem to be getting more disparate.

The overwhelming majority of people of every creed and colour are decent. Filth and murder lurk in dark corners within all society, where mercifully most of us don't tread. But when sexual predation or wanton violence surfaces it does so in such a blaze of publicity that we want to tar a whole race with the same brush. Mass retaliation, whether by word or deed, is unfair and not the answer, much as some of us want to lash out and gain disproportionate revenge. I see Asian kids on their way to school smiling and skipping, innocent youngsters who I sincerely hope will avoid the clutches of mind-altering lunatics who live by a creed formed from a few ill-chosen verses of a religious text. Seeing the innocence in a child's eyes is one of the great joys. It's only when we adults manipulate their minds that the smiles fade and suspicion and anger surface.

I'd set off in reasonable spirits but as my rumbling journey progresses the world around seeps in and spoils things a bit. It's not helped when a car of continental origin charges through a gap between parked, cars forcing me to test my brakes. The fat git sitting above and behind a four-ring badge waves a thank you as I am forced to give way – both of us know he had no intention of conceding. This little exchange is indicative of today's world – if you don't push, you rarely get off the start line. A frustrating little interlude for sure, which is soon put into perspective as I stop at a zebra crossing and allow a disabled man in a wheelchair to be pushed across the road.

To regain focus, I think of my upcoming project and how I will transform our house into a mini palace fit for my queen. Today I'm starting to build a wall in our bedroom, converting one third of our main bedroom into a bathroom. This will allow me to subsequently re-convert the existing (over-large) bathroom back into a third bedroom. The house was built around the turn of the twentieth century – three upstairs bedrooms, tin bath in the kitchen and outside bog. Simple days when convenience was not of primary concern. The chamber pots of that era now sprout house plants in the homes of the decor-conscious. Many of us are persuaded by large-breasted TV presenters that selling our home (for loads of grand) will only be achieved by scattering lavatorial accessories amid lurid colours.

Just for the record we have retained the outside loo (although it is now enclosed by a rather nasty wooden structure which I have cobbled together over the outside yard, optimistically called a workshop). Not only does my super-shed have its own lavatory, it also has a comfy chair near a cupboard where I keep a bottle of Grouse. It's a place to where I can retire after an unsuccessful disagreement with the management or contemplate my next renovation balls-up in comfortable, mind-dulled isolation.

I pull into the Builders Merchant's in my roof-racked SUV and park among the vans and trucks of rigger-booted tradesmen. One of the lads who works in the timber department pokes fun at my sandals. He asks if I want to borrow a pair of black socks to make me look a complete tosser. I'm forced to admit they're not the most apposite footwear for a builder - after all, dropping a breeze block on a non-steel-toe-capped foot is an unpleasant business. (My mate's wife calls them draught stones!)

My inappropriate uniform is matched only by my ignorance, but I'm learning all the time. I now know the distinction between, for example, scant, CLS or rough sawn timber and can request what I need with a modicum of authority. Previously I would walk around the timber shed, spot what looked like the right stuff and ask for 'some of that', then ask the footwear expert to chop it up into lengths that would go on my roof rack without it poking out over the front - to avoid turning myself into a jousting knight. The last thing I need is to return home with half a dozen natives skewered on my proboscis.

Actually, I've messed up. I've been distracted by the speech bubbles on the way in and quite forgotten I had to call in at the HSBC Bank in the centre of town. Consequently, I park in front of the town hall with a pile of timber on my roof rack. I seriously doubt my wood will be there when I return, following the inevitable row with a bank employee.

The reason I'm here? I've had to 'visit the local branch' to activate the keypad that allows me access to my Internet banking - so I can find out how little I have left. I had tried to do it online but one of the memorable answers wasn't recognized and they froze all my assets.

We were an hour and a half into my torment and they still hadn't sorted it out when one of life's older-age niggles surfaced. Annoyingly, my 60-year-old waterworks were in need of attention and I asked if I could use the lavatory. Turns out they don't have customer facilities in the bank so I had to walk a quarter of a mile up a hill and through a shopping centre in paint-splattered overalls. My sandals slapped on marble floors, drawing attention to my attire, as I rushed to find a public convenience. When I got there I found I needed a 20p coin to open the bloody turnstile to get in! I tried to explain to the yellow-jacketed cleaning attendant that my assets were frozen but he didn't understand the complications of high finance and was not for budging. I argued that 20p for a pee was a bit steep.

What would a stomach upset cost?

I was forced to hide and wait till he went on a tea break (not long) and I crawled under the barrier. No doubt I'll be on CCTV and a cardboard-heated council employee, sitting in front of a bank of TV screens, will inform the appropriate authorities. For the next few days I will wait, in a state of some agitation, to be arrested for gaining illegal entry into a public building. I rather hope my sandals don't give me away, because the rest of me looks like a real workman - one come to mend the turnstile perhaps?

I'd tweaked a calf muscle crawling under the barrier so limped back into the bank where we had to start again because of a 'system time-out.' Little sympathy was offered and I find it amazing how difficult it is to manage my own money. I was rather irate when things were finally resolved. I walked indignantly towards the exit.

'Could you spare a moment to complete a questionnaire about your banking experience?' asked a besuited, clackety-heeled young lady as I leave. 'Better not,' I tell her. I exit to find a traffic warden lurking near my lumber wagon. I'm actually still within the three-hour free parking limit, a limit they've obviously set with visits to the bank in mind. I make my way home through a minefield of roadworks, passing a very tidy grass verge and a man in a cloud. But at least its stopped raining so my damp wood might not warp too badly. I arrive with some optimism realizing that converting a house will be a doddle compared to venturing into the world beyond in my SUV.

Back to Our Roots

2019

… or more accurately, root vegetables. We've been back in Lancashire nearly four years. There have been ups and downs. Far more ups actually, but we find that the more we put in the more we get out, literally and figuratively. One thing's for sure, there's no need for inertia; there really is lots to do. For starters, there are plenty of events. Last week Littleborough brass band played in the park. Something like this is brilliant for the sloths among us because we don't have to do anything except get there. Just sit and listen. It was part of a 'Poppy River' event. Poppies are of course symbolic of the Great War, but people were invited to place a poppy in memory of a loved one who had not returned from any conflict. The red river flowed down the hill in the park from the children's playground. It continued past the bandstand and on into no-man's land beyond. Quite a sight it was, too. The band played a wonderfully tailored version of the Last Post and over a hundred people said a personal prayer in the sunshine.

Our return from a bohemian lifestyle to live within the hassle and frazzle of a modern world was an initial shock. A challenge to which we rose with our usual haphazard approach – basically, ignore what we can't change and trust to fate.

Bills and invoices landed on the mat with alarming regularity. Those that weren't chewed by the dog had to be settled. In order to pay them we had to work. But where does a nearly sixty-year-old git find gainful employment? There was a bit of cash coming in from the books I'd written but not enough to satisfy the blizzard of demands.

I've had no formal training but I'm OK with my hands. I've kitted out three boats after all. Unfortunately demand for canal boats is limited in central Littleborough. For some reason not many people wanted cassette toilets, three kilowatt inverters or marinised diesel engines. Folk are more concerned with getting their gardening or decorating done for as little as possible.

Budgetary relief came in the form of my step-branch of the family. They were moving up and up so I converted a garage into an office for them. Then I oversaw the renovation of a couple of houses they'd invested in. I enjoyed that so much (!*?) I did a further one for us. This meant actually laying out some of our own cash so the pressure was on a bit. In between, I built some fences, wooden garden adornments and various shelves and wardrobes. To be honest I was surprised how busy I'd become.

What is nice is chatting to the folk for whom I work. Some are a bit nervous at first; after all I'm untried and not yet trusted. That's in addition to being short of stature (compact), clothed to work (scruffy) and generally knackered-looking. One thing in my favour is my age. I'm perhaps perceived, by means of relative longevity and a reasonably middle-England accent, to be an upright citizen (although you'd question that after a day's work when I'm lying on the floor trying to re-organize various muscles). Also, I'm a local lad so can chat about the old days. (When we used to get proper blizzards.) This is rather fun because both me and my 'customers' are of a disposition where we've forgotten more than we remember. In fact, sometimes it's a voyage of discovery where we disinter buried memories long confined to a musty bottom draw. We can each talk utter balderdash because the other won't remember if it's fact or fiction. (Isn't disinter a funny-looking word?)

A couple of weeks ago I built a trellis for a lady. She lives in a house I used to visit fifty years ago. I'd go there to play with the children of a doctor who used to work with my dad. Between the lady and I, we pieced together fragments of then and now. It was all quite a pleasant coincidence but neither of us could remember the names of the children, just that at least one of them had ginger hair. It's like building a 3-D jigsaw where individual pieces are spread over both acreage and time. The nice thing is that the puzzle will never be finished; there is always something else to learn, another piece to fit.

Then there's the health, irregularities of which were uncovered during an old git's MOT. Everybody my age will have one complaint or other. This point in life seems to creep up and I'm sure I'm not alone pondering what more we might have done with our time. Or perhaps, just as importantly, what things we'd have been better off not doing. At the end of the day it is pretty irrelevant - we are where we are. For now I'm thankful that I can work and walk and write.

So, using two of those attributes, I walked to two local events yesterday and am now writing about them. Firstly, a heritage event celebrating Littleborough's special women. My wife spent the weekend in the company of three friends, all dressed as suffragettes. They variously waved placards demanding 'rights' and the vote. (Mind you, my wife had put our dinner in the slow cooker before she went out.)

It's surprising who you bump into. In a community house

in a town in the foothills of the Pennines I had a chat with a couple from Newcastle (upon Tyne) who were staying in their caravan on a small site near Sowerby Bridge. They must have entered, 'Women', 'downtrodden' and 'now what do we do'?' into an Internet search engine and come up with Hare Hill House, Littleborough. Quite whether they'd expected to get tangled up with a horde of noisy women in fancy dress is anyone's guess. But their alternative this particular Sunday was the Great North Run in their home town. 'Not likely,' the chap said.

One of the women we celebrated was midwife to Littleborough from around 1930. She was a wonderful lady called Ivy Ellis who was little short of a heroine to many local families. Roughly twenty years before the NHS was formed (in 1948, 5th July to be precise), she would have battled all weathers to help expectant mums, sometimes arriving on horse and cart. With little more than a few towels, warm water and a fire in the grate, many local folk made their entrance. Through one of Ivy's relatives, we had access to her photograph album. Photos of some fifty babies spanning twenty years were displayed during this heritage celebration. Many of the names are familiar and some of the tots of yesteryear will be the forebears of today's generation.

The second event was the Hare Hill Allotment Show. I've actually done a fair amount of work one way or another around the allotments, building sheds and fences for example, even a chicken run (some wag named it Cluckingham Palace). Consequently, I was keen to show my support for a healthy and popular activity. I've seen many workers upended in the undergrowth, tending their crops, so I was interested to see the results.

It was being held in Littleborough Coach House and Heritage Centre, which according to the blurb *'is a Grade 2 Listed building of architectural and historical interest within an important conserva-*

tion area. Dating from the late 18th century, it was originally built to serve the Bury horse-drawn coach traffic on the main transport routes into Yorkshire across Blackstone Edge.' (There, a bit of culture at last!)

The first thing of note is that the show was upstairs, rather unkind on the exhibitors who had to lump their wares up a floor - some of the fruit and veg on display was of considerable size. There is a lift mind, but I ignored it and staggered up the stairs, keen to demonstrate my physical prowess. I arrived at the registration desk in a state of some distress. I found out later that the lift has the reputation of being unpredictable, in that it can stop when it feels like it or the doors fail to open. The thought of spending the night in an enclosed space with a sack of misshapen vegetables is worrisome indeed. At least one shouldn't starve.

On arrival at the registration desk, I was instantly relieved of a pound (the official visitor's entry fee) by the daughter-in-law of the man who used to help us in our garden forty years ago. He was called Reg Philpott – a splendid name for a gardener. What a nice man he was too. Barely had my coin landed in the re-purposed ice cream carton, than I was relieved of a further pound for a raffle ticket. I could win a tempting basket of delicacies, a large proportion of which have come from the Coop. This seemed rather incongruous when there was so much fresh produce not ten feet away in the display hall.

'Right, thank you,' I said, and set off to the right, towards the exhibits. This was the familiar direction my wife and I have taken on a number of occasions when we have given our slideshow talks to various local groups. But I was thwarted ...

'Er, this way please.'

I was herded to the left, towards the tombola where I am

relieved of another pound by the granddaughter of the daughter-in-law of the man who used to help us in our garden forty years ago. See, I can add another piece to our local jigsaw. She is a polite, bright young thing who has been carefully schooled in the art of relieving pounds from passing vegetable enthusiasts. Who can resist a pretty smile and a table full of goodies?

I'm not normally lucky with tombolas but that day I was. But I didn't win a 'goody,' I won a spiky plant in a paper cup called a septum (or something like that). My wife, I am sure, is overwhelmed by my good fortune, if not the state of our finances.

At last I was in. Three room-long tables bore the fruits of the allotmenteers labours. Impressive they were too. Pumpkins, onions, carrots, raspberries, apples etc. Some of which were enormous and all of it looking fresh-from-the-sod healthy.

A friend of mine and her associate were loitering.

The associate persuaded me to partake of the gardening quiz. Another pound – 'only.' I had taken the precaution of calling at the hole-in-the-wall en route from the suffragettes. Good job, because I could easily have been financially embarrassed.

I could answer so few quiz questions it was hardly worth me borrowing a pen. I only got two correct for certain. One was, 'Who was Bill and Ben's friend in the 1960s TV show?' and the other was a photograph that I identified of a shell-less terrestrial gastropod mollusc. Weed and slug were my correct answers – which rather gives you a clue as to my gardening capabilities.

There was just time for me to be relieved of a further two pounds for some delicious-looking tomatoes and green beans. To be fair, I potentially has something to show for all the money I'd 'invested.' I won a prickly thing on the tombola, I might win the raffle, I might win the quiz (though that was unlikely, unless nobody else entered) and I had some lovely produce. I include the entry fee here because I have enjoyed chatting, looking and admiring.

Most important of all I have joined in. There really is no excuse for 'having nothing to do' or being bored or lonely. There are all sorts of things to get involved with, new folks to meet, activities to try and jigsaws to complete. Community – it's what small towns like Littleborough thrive on, have done for centuries. Ours seems to be doing very nicely, thank you.

Post Apocalypse

2022

No, that doesn't refer to a postal strike, it's that damn pandemic. Which I'm not going to mention! The beauty of literary license is that I can add a few minutes here, a day there or completely ignore the two years when the world went mad. What I can do is share my joy at watching our town come back to life. Frankly, I'm lucky to have survived the last two years, not because of the virus, but because my poor wife was locked up in a bungalow with me. How on earth she didn't clack me over the head with a frying pan is anybody's guess. Living within the confines of a boat was good preparation for our landlocked incarceration.

We're starting to do normal things again, some pleasant, some less so. In the latter category, dental check-ups. My dentist is a serious person. If I crack a silly joke, he just stares into the abandoned building site that is my mouth - and frowns.

'It can't be that bad,' I say. 'Can it?'

He turns and mutters something to his assistant, in what could be Urdu.

My Urdu is a bit sketchy, but I reckon he says something like, 'Pass me the 'last resort syringe' - let's shut this bozo up for a while.'

I came in feeling reasonably jolly. Now, flat on my back at the mercy of my dour dentist, I'm thinking I should have made up an excuse and gone shopping instead. He's a modern professional, rather 'way of the world' in his behaviour. In other words, speedy, efficient and slightly remote. Not at all like my previous dentists. My childhood one was jolly but fearsome. He could have played a malevolent Father Christmas in a Stephen King novel. His surgery was at the top of a dim stairway. He used to knock me out to do extractions – yes, full anaesthetic with gas. To this day I wake in a cold sweat at the thought of being asphyxiated by that damn mask. My next dentist operated out of a converted cow shed in the Shropshire countryside. Nice guy, and if he hadn't had complete control over me psychologically and orally, we could have been friends.

As I drive away from today's dentist, with oral discomfort I hadn't had when I arrived, I pass the Sun Hotel which has seen better days. In the dim and distant past, we used to join their excellent quiz nights. In fact, quite by chance I met the former landlady recently at the bowling club. It was nice to reminisce – she's a fun lady – but a shame that such good days are now confined to a memory.

Bowling club folk are mainly 'of an age.' No disrespect intended but, like Rudolf, 'I've joined in their games' recently and found a nice bunch of people. The thing is that the senior generation, of which I'm knocking on the door, are the ones who will remember the gentler, less fraught times of half a century ago.

Occasionally I come across someone with a direct link to my family, in particular my father, who died fifty years ago. One thing that chokes me up more than anything is the possibility that people I see walking our streets, or riding a bus, or sitting by the bowling green, may have been made well by my Dad. He was a doctor who cured many but was unable to help himself.

I met a guy recently who put the central heating system in our house when I was two years old. He'd have seen me at my absolute best - it was all a bit of a shambles after that! Two days later, I learned that my neighbour, a former nurse (then a student) worked with my dad at the local hospital (Birch Hill) and later nursed him as he died. Amazingly, she lives two doors from me. Though we're friends, neither of us were aware of my family connection. More pieces of my jigsaw go in.

One thing of which I am very proud is that my Godmother, Marjorie Barker, gifted five acres of land to the town in memory of her husband Edmund, my Uncle Teddy. Since 1990, Barker's Wood, partly thanks to schoolchildren who planted trees, has matured into a lovely community woodland. I know folk of all ages enjoy it and what a terrific legacy to leave behind. She was a wonderful lady, among many of that generation. Contrast that with the seemingly endless building, turning open land into housing estates for people we can't support. I used to play in the field that's now Barker's Wood as a child and just across the brook was Dearnley School (where I started my educational decline!). That's gone, too, in favour of a Kingdom Hall. So you see, my psyche, and that of my family is rooted in this town.

But, while I dream of things historical, one nagging little difficulty has just surfaced in the present. It must be the excitement of the dentist, and my survival therein, but the alarm has gone off on a bodily function. The diminishing efficiency of my ageing waterworks has inconveniently coincided with the decline of public toilets. A public inconvenience indeed. So, rather than dash off to buy some budget jogging bottoms, I'm forced to return home, were I'll find a flushing lavatory - with a bit of luck. These days, sorties have to be planned. There has to be a drinks amnesty before travel combined with careful onward planning.

Before I discovered the bowling club, the dentist was the only 'exciting' thing I had lined up post-apocalypse, which is a bit sad. My wife is better organized. She colours her hair pink and dives right back into her assortment of social delights. Townswomen's Guild, art groups, the historical society. Mind you, her going out means I can watch a man film without feeling guilty. Action, not smut!

The Brass Band is back. Sundays have just not been the same. The silence sat heavy over the park like a 1960s smog. But once again stirring music echoes back from the nearby houses, built on the site of a former factory that went up in a spectacular blaze not long ago. Thumping tunes roll out across the park and playing fields. Have the rhododendrons put on a special display this year? As I sit and listen, I'm reminded of playing tennis on the grass courts the far side of the kiddies' playground. Like other people, I thought I was a world-beater when Wimbledon was on TV.

While listening to the band, Jan is chatting with a friend who moans, 'My runner beans are not doing at all well.'

'Oh good,' says Jan.

'I beg your pardon?'

'It's not just ours that have failed then.'

Yes, everything is blooming. Except our runner beans. And those of Jan's friend. The sap is up, the grass is green, but our beans are not at all well. Some have surfaced but look like they've been strafed by a Spitfire, others have been nibbled by malicious molluscs. Many have stayed below decks altogether. I go out at every opportunity to stare at the skeletal bamboo frame atop the bed and hope for a miracle. I think I need help from the experts in the allotments.

Prices seem to have nudged upwards, obviously from twenty-five years ago, but recent increases seem to be exponential. I bought a leg of lamb for my birthday treat back in February and couldn't believe the price. 'Diesel's gone up,' said the butcher. 'I thought sheep ran on grass!' Fleeced, that's what I was. But I paid up and enjoyed what may be my last ever leg of lamb.

Recently there was a food festival. The occasion reinforced the notion that our appetite for foodstuffs and frolic is undiminished. Indeed, food and drink are go-to escapes when things get fraught. Stomachs swell and boozy brains become befuddled when there's angst about. Our high street (that's called a road) was closed off to traffic to make way for a variety of stalls. Lovely smells and happy chatter filled the air. Goodness knows where all the cars were parked, those that normally park on the pavements. We bought some local wine and local cheese and some sausage from Poland. Locals, sensible in their professional lives, acted daft and flogged raffle tickets and balloons. Our next generation thumped out brassy tunes on the back of a lorry to the pride of their families and the pleasure of all. Great stuff.

In this money-mad, material world the richest prize of all is companionship. Two recently formed groups are helping local folk rediscover just that. First, *Blokes*, where a bevy of men gather for company and friendship. With the group came The Golden Gnome, their official mascot. It's a statue about the size of an Oscar, only far more valuable. I was asked by the head bloke, the man who conceived the idea, to attend the very first meeting 'in case we are short of numbers.' Later he said, 'You don't need to come again.' People, it seems, wanted, needed, cherished company. A replica gnome is awarded monthly to a member recognized for special service to the gathering. 'Special Service?' Well, that's cake-making or washing-up or domino-shuffling or pie-eating or just turning up.

Then, two ladies recently started a support/social group called *Chill and Chat.* Friendship and caring cure so many ills. I have to say there is a much better chance of the ladies solving world crises; the blokes appear too busy playing dominoes and eating cake! They are both proper community events, each started by people who remember when 'community' was the focal point of village life rather than an optional extra.

What I will add is that two of the facilitators have excellent reasons for starting their groups. Both have come through very difficult times and received much-needed help to get through. They both, independently, wanted to give something back. That something became somewhere - a place where people could find an open door, a smile, friendship and a warm welcome. Oh, and very likely, a piece of cake.

What the two-year hiatus did was make us realize how much we miss the simple things, largely revolving around personal interaction. Things we took for granted like chatting in a café or having meal out. Friendship the common denominator.

Since my return a couple of nagging anomalies have cropped up. Twenty-five years ago, I took good health pretty much for granted. I would run for the bus, now I wait for the next one. Daft as it sounds, I have to exercise to stand still. To 'not get any worse' in other words. Luckily, I enjoy power walking. I'm huffing and puffing one day, severely testing my abilities, when my friend leans over his garden wall and describes my walking style as 'pedestrian.' He's 80+ with new knees. Five years ago, walking was an ordeal; now, with plenty of practice, it's merely uncomfortable – another couple of decades and I'll be jogging.

Energy was in ample supply back in my early teens. Despite that, a game of golf entailed a protracted effort. A half a mile walk from home, then the bus into Littleborough centre, followed by the train to Todmorden and finally a walk from Tod station to the golf club up on Cross Stone (a good mile, half up a very steep hill). Me and my mate would play 36 holes, then I'd do the journey in reverse. Then the following day, then the next ... These days I watch golf on telly and need a refresher after nine holes.

Yes, activity is important - in my case, walking and cycling. I recently added snooker to my fitness regime. It's not just waggling one arm about; I have to march round the table picking my brother's balls out, if you will. He's better than me, in fact so much so that I ended up utterly humiliated, particularly when we were being watched by the builder lads who'd come in for a pint. We even changed tables so I couldn't be spied on and guffawed at, but they just turned round and watched from a bit further away. So, rather than knuckle down, concentrate and put in hours of practice, I gave up altogether. I now watch *Flog It* instead and the snooker cue is in the garden supporting some raspberries. Which probably won't grow.

Go On Then, One More

2022 (still)

I lied earlier - I will mention the 'P' word again because, among the madness, there were some amusing happenings. 'Why are Nanny Janny and Papa Jo sideways, Mummy?' asks number one grandson, using our official family names. 'I'm not sure to be honest,' replies Mum.

We are on a Zoom call with Grandsons one and two and Mum. The grandparents mastery of things technical is poor. Thus, our image appears at right angles. It's our fault, nothing to do with the younger generations. The lads have been having home-schooling and are keen and bright. Now the sight of Papa Jo drinking a mug of tea at right angles threatens to undo all the rudimentary physics they've been taught.

When we departed the borough thirty plus years ago, portable telephones were the size of a brick. Now we can talk in real time on any number of gadgets, even if we are perpendicular to the word.

There's a field outside our house and over the last couple of years, we witnessed a dog explosion - which paints a rather nasty picture! Remember to begin with we were only allowed out for specific reasons, one of them to walk a dog? Well, the same dog would walk past time after time attached to different people. Let's call him Dougal, in honour of the star of *The Magic Roundabout*. Dougal spent many years going round in circles arguing with Ermintrude and Dylan. He started out tall and gangly like a greyhound but ended up like, well Dougal, with his stomach scraping the floor. Modern day Dougal, poor thing, was dragged round and round ploughing an increasingly deep furrow.

Eventually, those overworked dogs were pensioned off so people bought a new one instead, often at vastly inflated prices. So, rather than one dog between twenty, it became a dog each. We were privileged to witness a bewildering assortment of training regimes, from intensive to nil. There were shouts and whistles and clapping and some bad language. Some dogs set off after a ball, ignored the 'fetch' command and disappeared over the horizon. Internet listing a few hours later, 'Lost. Dog that doesn't answer to the name of Chardonnay.'

Other dogs hurtled around trailing training leads. Ten metres of snappy, writhing canvas following manic young dogs, like a herd (or rhumba) of angry rattlesnakes in a pit. One such lead got tangled round my legs as an out-of-control mutt charged around in ever decreasing circles. I had a firm word with the detached owner (who was blowing furiously on a dog-whistle) as she told me proudly, 'This is how you're supposed to train them.'

One walk per day was the Government diktat - was that maximum or minimum? Whichever, dogless people lumbered past too. The thing is, some of them hadn't moved out of their armchairs for forty years; now, released from their recliners, they were marching around like someone frantically searching for the last toilet roll.

Our garden got revamped. All the successful bits I could pat myself on the back for. All the bits that did not go so well, like parsley and mangetout peas, I blamed on the virus. Three-quarters of a box of very expensive bulbs and plants, bought off the Internet and delivered in a huge 10-tonne truck, went into the soil and simply disappeared. What do you do? I could hardly send them back. They came from a garden centre in Kent, some 300 miles distant, and no doubt they would have blamed my incompetence.

Then there was a 'special' plant given to us by my step-daughter, a euphorbia. Phonetically, "You for Beer." Sounds encouraging, but wine is my tipple. In fact, it's name has a rather pleasant gardening feel about it - Euphoria with a 'b' in it! However, this species is one of mixed blessings. As well as being a potential cure for skin cancer, one poisonous seed can kill a child. If handled without gloves it can cause a nasty rash, but they are also described as easy to grow with few problems! So, slightly nervous and wearing gloves, I planted the healthy specimen. There was a good 8 - 12 inches poking above ground in the form of rich green leaves. Within 2 days it had disappeared altogether, never to be seen again. I have mixed feelings about its absence. I have the suspicion, that had it thrived, either my wife or me (or the dog) may have been injured! I blame its disappearance on Brexit.

One place people walked was Hollingworth Lake. A century and a half ago, the lake was deep within a 3,000 foot volcano, but the erosive action of millions of shuffling footsteps has worn the pathway to barely 5 feet above water level. There's a press release towards the end of the book that fleshes out the lake's story.

Cycling is another thing that has boomed. Fifty years ago,

I was knocked off my bike at the bottom of Wardle Road by a man called Mr Carson driving a steamed-up Volkswagen Beetle. Bit unlucky, really, because there were only about four cars in Lancashire back then. Fast forward and even getting off your driveway these days is to dice with death. Boy, oh boy, is it busy!

Nevertheless, I was inspired to buy a bike. It's wonderful and I haven't looked back since (largely because if I did I'd end up in the canal). It's an e-bike, imported from Korea by the company that supplies the chap who runs the bike shop in Littleborough. So, by the time I get it, a few people have added a percentage and it's quite pricey. He's a good man though, is Paul. I had to wait six weeks because the thousands of people who'd bought new dogs also bought new bikes and there was a shortage. Of course, e-bikes are a recent innovation, as are e-scooters and e-cars. Mind you, e-milk floats have been around a while.

During my cycle research I went to have a look in Halfords which, due to a resurgence in the popularity of cycling, was nearly empty of stock. If I'd wanted a non-electric, pink, ladies bike or something with stabilizers for a three-year-old, I was in luck. But there was nothing to suit me, so I wandered round the empty warehouse trying to look like an athlete.

My e-bike, though not cheap, was worth waiting for. I've had some exciting experiences already, and most of those have involved trying to clamber into my new cycle shorts without getting cramp. The relaunch of my cycling career was almost as well attended as the launch of the final space shuttle, with a similar amount of steam coming out of the bottom. Mind you, my very first trial run, round the snooker club car park, resulted in an injury within one yard – literally. The handlebars are much wider than anything I've ridden before, so I scraped my hand on the stone wall while initiating the launch procedure.

I've written a book called *A Bike at Large* which catalogues the cycling ordeals of a man in his early 60s with a health issue or two. My cycling saga is the antidote to the beautiful, glossy cycling magazines that feature svelte, bronzed gods on expensive machinery. Let's be honest, few of us will look as good as the beautiful people in the mags. Me? I'm a blob in a green jacket getting myself in a right old mess. If you can waddle on a bike, I do it.

On a positive note, we managed to offload our horrid old car in favour of a French thing that's so full of gadgets you need a degree in electronics to start the damn thing. But it's large enough to hold my bike, various cycling accessories, me, Jan, some luggage, and provisions for a day out. Plus the dog in his cage.

We bought the car specifically to take day trips with all the family. However, the first 'test run' didn't go well. We piled everything in and set off for Clitheroe. Why? Well, we liked the sound of the place and we'd never been. Anyhow, the car performed fine, but the outing hit a sour note when we discovered the dog had vomited on the picnic hamper. Poor lad isn't used to a smooth ride and folding seats. But in all fairness, he's a very considerate vomiter, surreptitious and private, not like a tiger roaring out of the undergrowth. As you can imagine, that was an appetite suppressant. Undeterred we moved on to Lytham where we had a walk down the prom in sub-zero temperatures. For nourishment we had a lump of cheese and a horrendous coffee from a petrol station before heading home to clean the car.

We left Littleborough in the relative comfort of a Ford Granada. We returned thirty years later in a camper van that was probably being built as we left - an ancient Talbot that was our home for a few months while we looked for a house. This was a mini-adventure in itself, seeking out quirky, out-of-the-way little camp sites. Such as one in Lees where the pitches are in the garden of a former pub. There was space for about 10 vans; it was dog friendly and there was a pub across the road. Another was The Halifax Steam Brewing Company in Hipperholme, serviced by it's 'tap room' called the Cock-o' the North. Needless to say we enjoyed a couple of nights there. We'd cruised in the underbelly of northern England camper-vanning. It's surprising what lurks in little-known corners.

Hordes of people have moved onto fields around our town where they have conveniently built houses. Convenient for the incomers that is, not so much for the wildlife. Meanwhile a branch of our family has moved out, up to the Howgill Fells in Cumbria. I'd never heard of the area. It's between the Lakes and the Yorkshire Dales and is great walking and cycling territory, though don't even consider visiting with a dicky battery - its hilly! What's that got to do with Littleborough? They used to live here. Tenuous but accurate.

I bumped into a childhood friend the other day. He's a lad with whom I used to go sniggling or swaling. Remember? Setting fire to grass. The irony is that we'd set puny, mini blazes right on the spot where I'd later live with my wife on Laburnum Way, Bents Farm. My mate later joined the Fire Brigade. Sniggler to fire-fighter is probably a career progression explained deep within the works of Freud or Socrates. There wasn't a single house on Bents Farm back then, just fields all the way down to Cecil Street.

We can't fail to notice food delivery services zipping about on scooters. All geared up to ordering your takeaway with minimal effort. Armchair to front door and back to armchair. No exercise, no social contact. Would we have used these services had they been available? Yes, probably! Instead, forty years ago, I remember helping my mum do *Meals on Wheels*. We'd pick up insulated boxes full of trays of hot meals from Birch Hill's kitchen. I have to say it always smelled good. I remember Christmas day specifically, when we'd visit people who would not otherwise have a Christmas dinner. Mum and I may well be the only people these folk saw on Christmas day. Many of them had prepared a tray with a bottle of sherry or whiskey so we could share a tipple with them. After a dozen or so visits I was barely in a fit state to drive, but I do remember the smiles on the faces of the folk. That, I can tell you, is a very warm memory.

I think the older we get, the more we cherish the past. We cherry-pick, of course, by remembering the happy bits we consign the dross to our unconscious. This little book is just a bunch of personal recollections, largely daft. Often, as in the book's tag line, it compares now and then. I'm sure some of you will recognize historical bits, but you'll also have your own good memories to look back on (and bad bits to recall if you need to).

Thing is, we can't change the past, but we can make the most of today. In the blink of an eye we'll be relying on what we've done today to help us through those wrinkly armchair years.

So, best not mess it up.

There follow two tongue-in-cheek press releases. They may offer a suggestion as to how we'll leave the Boro for future generations.

STOP PRESS

The LankyArchaeology Society was formed in 3008.

LankyArchaeology Society
PRESS RELEASE

For immediate release
December 6th 3020.

A series of cave paintings has been discovered on the outskirts of the former settlement of Littleborough. The township sunk into the mud around 900 years ago when the sub-soil was unable to support the weight of a government-sponsored building programme. The paintings were found in a derelict visitor centre and depict tantalising evidence of an inland body of water.

The paintings were somewhat degraded after around 1000 years in the northern climate. Local weather patterns were described by natives in the early 21st century as ***shite***.

The indigenous people hereabouts used a peculiar dialect call Romancashire. Translations of the painted texts indicate the lake was known colloquially as:

Aqueous decies centena imagini nil focusum

A rather wordy description translated as:

Lake of a million blurred photographs.

The lake is located within the crater of an extinct volcano, the sides of which are estimated to have originally risen to a height of around 3000 ft.

The artwork depicts local people trudging round and round the lake perimeter, over a period of a number of years, often with a thousand-yard stare, sometimes dragging unwilling, domesticated animals. Over aeons the walls of the volcano were eroded by this constant marching. By the time the borough disappeared, the pathway was almost at water level.

One further conundrum indicated by the paintings is discussion about a freedom of movement policy called *'Right to Roam.'* This perversely appears to have coincided with a building programme designed to cover every blade of grass with concrete.

There's no longer lake of course - the crater was filled in around 2,500 AD.

Ends:-

****

LankyArchaeology Society
PRESS RELEASE

For immediate release
March 7th 3021.

During reconstruction of a high-speed scooter/cycle/ hover track, archaeologists have uncovered evidence of a former waterway. An ancient tablet, discovered nearby, sheds light on the discovery.

When deciphered from the local Romancashire dialect, the tablet made reference to the mysterious name of the waterway, **One Hundred Anal**, abbreviated to **C. Anal**.

Archaeologists believe that the watercourse was used as some sort of ancient sewer, hence the 'Anal' reference.

The mystery deepened when evidence of stool-like objects was discovered on the path which ran alongside the sewer. So, why was the path used to dispose of waste products and not the sewer itself? A mystery indeed.

In addition, stools, carefully packaged in small plastic casks, were discovered in petrified bushes by the side of the C. Anal.

This aspect of the mystery appears to have been solved by

translation of the following sentence on the ancient tablet:

Valet stercus unus ex duobus viam in rubo

which translates as:

A turd on the path is worth two in the bush

The use of plastic stool sacks was extensive. It appears that our ancient ancestors also threw the plastic sacks in the long grass in times of fruitful harvest. When the foliage died back in the winter, numerous plastic bags could be seen littering the landscape. When analysed, the contents of these sacks seems to indicate that the wolf-like creatures of the period, probably domesticated, thrived largely on a diet of horse-meat.

Fortunately for us in the year 3021, the plastic sacks are perfectly preserved (plastic has an undetermined half-life, many millennia for certain) so we were able to identify the stools.

We at the LankyArchaeology Society are still trying to unravel the revolting habits of our ancestors.

Plastic was superseded by bamboo roughly nine-hundred years ago but thanks to plastic we have uncovered a fascinating, if nasty, ancestral trait.

Ends:-

About the Author

I live in Littleborough with my wife Janna and dog Tache.

We've both lived here on and off for over 60 years.

I began writing monthly articles for a canal magazine in 2007. Catastrophically (for the magazine), following an editorial misunderstanding, we parted company. Yes, I was sacked. I began to chronicle our travels which ultimately resulted in my three 'At Large' books, beginning with *'A Narrowboat at Large.'* I describe the books as a huge collection of warm memories, a library on which Jan and I can draw during long winter evenings and which will help us through our rocking-chair years. Magical times.

After destroying the UK's canal infrastructure on two narrowboats and rearranging a fair amount of continental waterways heritage on a rusty old Dutch Barge, our boating days came to an end in 2015, to everyone's relief except ours.

Boating days behind me, my new challenge is an e-bike. However, to mix metaphors, it's not all been plain sailing. *A Bike at Large* is written in homage to all portly, sub-standard cyclists, of which I am one. *Ordeals on Wheels* sums it up quite nicely.

I've also written three novels in addition to this little book of memories.

You can connect with me on:

- https://jomay.uk
- https://www.facebook.com/jotheboat

Also by Jo May

Before this mini book, I've written 7 others.

My 'At Large' series comprises three boating books and a cycling one:
- A Narrowboat at Large (below)
- A Barge at Large
- A Barge at Large II
- A Bike at Large

Three novels:
- Operation Vegetable
- Twice Removed
- Flawed Liaisons

They are all here on my website: jomay.uk

A Narrowboat at Large

So why did we take to the water? My wife can't swim, the dog hates it and I prefer beer. Financially we were afloat and we lived in a perfectly decent house until my wife came up with the zany idea of living on a boat.

Amazing really, a couple of years later, we'd sold the house and moved onto our first narrowboat.

It was July 4th 2003. Independence Day

Printed in Great Britain
by Amazon